GARETH WRITER-DAVIES

Wysg

ARENIG PRESS

First published in 2022
by Arenig Press
Fedw Fawr, Llwynygroes, Tregaron SY25 6QF

Printed in UK by
4Edge.co.uk

A CIP record for this book
is available from the British Library

ISBN : 978-1-9998491-7-7

Cover: Map of Monmouthshire
engraved by William Blaeu Circa 1645
IM Fell English font digitally reproduced by Igino Marini.
www.iginomarini.com

ink drawings by Rachael Writer-Davies

To Martin & Keri

Previous Publication

Some of these poems were previously published within the following magazines:

Ink, Sweat and Tears
The Writer's Centre Magazine
Runcible Spoon
Guillemot Press
Spelt
Nine Muses
Confluence
The 7th Quarry
A New Ulster
Allegro Poetry
Frangipani Press
Live Encounters
Algebra of Owls
14 Magazine
Three Drops from a Cauldron
Slim Anthology (Three Drops from a Cauldron)
Lyadora Anthology
The High Window
Poetry Village (when 5G titled 4G)
Poems of Adventure
Foxglove Journal
A470 Anthology (Arachne)
Rosemary McLeish Poetry Prize Anthology 2021
Owls-Shortlisted for Welshpool Poetry Competition 2019
Otters-Highly Commended Welsh Poetry Competition 2017

Contents

Cath
Lay-By, A470, Storey Arms Pass
Standing Stone
Hess
5G
Pen y Fan
Windflowers
Here
Old Fools Are Babes Again
Water

Wysg

Water Under the Bridge

when I first moved
here

I was entranced (if that's the right word
perhaps)
by the river passing by

and when in February
the river was wild

I thought *what have I done*
will I get out of here
alive?

the river sped
with all the fishy dross of time

now
I take the river as it runs
high
low
its tumbling murmurations (never two the same)

and rather than sticking to the navigation
of my intended line
I study the flow

charmed/horrified
by was and is and what will be mine

so hard
to hold a moment of water in your hands

I wake after rain
the river rattling like a crow

it's come to take me
and to let me go

Waterfall

in Spring
the waterfall can throw its voice
three yards in an impressive arc of vigour

in Summer
distracted by nesting birds
the waterfall narrows and dribbles

in Autumn
thirsty sheep are extracted
and the waterfall becomes a cacophony of glass baubles

in Winter
the waterfall gathers
and gushes over the lip with an operatic tour de force (*in bocca al lupo*)

The Cutters

It's the clatter I hear first
of metal tooth biting down
scything sharp through the wildings.

The most stupid way to die
is flaying by hedge cutter.
So I wave my arms and jump

and the two farmboys with grins
like soldiers pause the grinders
in mid-air like *Transformers*.

I keep eye contact and smile
in case they have a pungent
sense of humour and slam-drop

the reapers within a touch
of my head to watch me quake
like a lamb from a dragon.

I hedge past and they re-start
tearing maythorn and elder
twisting and bending edges

taming the passing season.
I quicken and nose my path
disappear into the green.

Sheep

even
as I look
the flat eyes of the sheep

size me up
as if
I am the carcass hanging from a hook

strayed
from the fold of the map
lost

within the contours
I happened
upon the flock

who even as I look
chew
the cud and do not break

knowing
I am no good shepherd
able

with words
to turn
silence into tractability

but a stranger
come far
without a dog

maybe
I am less than death
a gasp

a shadow
waiting by the brook
the sheep

stamp their hooves
baulk
not to be deceived again

Almost

missing I am   those words
words
in shops and passing words

that are almost   not language
a flex
of the muscle   of the palate

a ruler on the tongue
I miss
sullen vowels sudden   consonants

words
I hung upon a hook
like a coat too heavy for the season

whilst I chose something lighter
that almost
fitted

& used my teeth for speaking
I could not tell
how I was feeling

words
knotted
have I not saying

the ear is almost a tongue
the eye also
articulate   define

Snow

at Pavlova, Crickhowell (looking for early signs of my dementia)

it's cosy in here
my seat next to the window
snow adding itself to the snowy trees

I have been day-sleeping (half in love)
like a nightingale

and the flags
make me drowsy
as I watch the snow fall, upon the ha-ha-ha of the town

I have little more to say upon the subject of snow
I may have something to say, later

Owls
The Groves, Brecon

I trust nothing
that flies at night, with atropine eyes and a sense of purpose

owls fly certainly, like popes
birds of the imagination

though cuter than bats
still they rip the heads from mice and puke guts into fledgers

in all innocence
I am lurking in the Groves at midnight

and all around me, the animal kingdom
is having sex, truffling, making good their nests

whilst I am only
upon paths that were vague in daylight and now uncertain

what is mud, what is concrete
what moves in silence, as I hitch flight on the obscure, ambiguous

design, now mediated
like wood that drifts down a river or a stone that sparks

I stand here, clothed in the dark other
not to be trusted, with the old knowledge of kill or be killed

Tooth & Claw

the house reeks of rotting rats
which I guess is progress

they had gotten bold
chewing through infrastructure, infesting the cavities

and like family
who can outstay a pre-arranged welcome

nature is enough, through the window
too much, when sharing your home

and to trap the bait
in well travelled passageways

was a friendly kind
of slaughter

now alone, I re-take my home
incense masks brutal nature

one must be the master
rats are not beautiful

Teeth

everyone is nice (at least that should be the assumption)
nice
until proven otherwise

don't be too hasty
but
don't be too naïve

thinking
a smile (pearly white)
has no side to it

animals bare their teeth
before
they attack

Eels

I lie by the river
watching the glass eels with electromagnetic radiation

when the Romans came to Wales there was no system of days
only the sun coming up and the sun going down

I lie by the river with my nets and my traps
waiting

a barometer and GPS
the two questions of life; what's the weather and where are we going?

A Clergyman Clears a Drain in a Lonely Welsh Valley

There's nothing quite so satisfying
as finding a blocked drain
and freeing the grid of leaves and muck

with a boot and rod to get the slack water flowing.
That great suck of gravity
as the froth of mulch   clings   then plunges.

Under the barbed hedge the quaggy water swirls
then races towards the church
tarmac just another way for water to get where it is going.

My liturgical heel does its good deed
as I pry my collar
cock my ear and mouth the words of the psalter.

Alone in my anorak and biretta
the wind like a wild mane   the waters rising once again.

St. Simon & St. Jude
Llanddeusant, in the shadow of the Black Mountain

they make a singular team
the zealot and the saint of lost causes

Simon being one of the vaguer apostles
and Jude no better

than one who hangs around with the boys
for his own (obscure) reasons

like many odd couples
there's a whimsical symmetry to their histories

of death by tools
and dearth of miracles precursing

like a reminder
that even the most unsung of lives is worthy of canon

A Fatal Mistake

I thought a pauper's grave and no one to remember me
was the way to go

having read a Hardy novel
where as usual the wheel of fate turns upon a small past error

this modest proposal of obliteration
seemed pleasingly dramatic and tidied up any loose ends

my sins have been few
and my daughters play in the garden

turning cartwheels
as if nothing in the world could ever go wrong

I nap
page three hundred and twenty open in my lap

and wake
buried in an unmarked grave and forgotten thoroughly

Artificial Islands

amongst midges and the roots of mud sucking reeds
I am searching

for arrow heads
and any other signs

that the largest body of water in Brycheiniog
once

held castles
floating upon islands of thatch

the tideless water
giving man everything he needed

trout
a raft of ones own

and the ability to punt to another acre of lake
brazenly declare

a kingdom
amongst the rushes like a bronze age Robinson Crusoe

bowed and arrowed
the cautionary display of your neighbour's head upon a spike

Ode to a Great Egret
Llyn Syfaddon

wings
like piston rods
neck
a sprung Z
like the last fold
of an *orizuru*

a quill
made from a penna

the alders shake
as you leap

white space

feather
by feather

like the index
of a book
a veil
a bridal dress

cuk cuk-ing
like a spoke-card

wire   glue

a paper aeroplane
a glass
of spilt milk

where to you flying?

Knight, Knight
St Edmund's Church, Crickhowell

by the altar
Herbert leans on an elbow and raises a casual knee

swathed in rough chained filigree
as if
in a jocular moment between feud and combat

he popped
into the waiting niche

and was overcome
by sleep

stone cold
he lies
like a rude memorial to the sudden coming of death

aslumber
in his petrification of seven hundred years and two thousand sermons

he dreams
of the sun rising upon the vasty fields of Agincourt

Kurosawa
Tretower Court

the fortified house is built around a square, with sloping
rooves and a balcony tied into the eaves

rain drips from the tiles
and in the courtyard, the tethered horses steam

I am here to admire the medieval hall of dragons
and through the hatched windows

the ruined castle is picturesque, as on cue blue sky appears
over Bwlch

but my mind, is occupied by samurai
the long death of Toshiro Mifune, in a cloud-burst of arrows

I should be thinking of Welsh princes
and the thousand year struggle with the bloody English

maybe, I have a lack of *hiraeth*
and find it easier to side with a rising sun

the rain returns
the scene fades to black and white

and as the horses are unleashed
I hear a small voice call "action"

ready to die, a hundred samurai ride out
banners unfurled, swords sharpened, breathing fire

The Garden
Open Gardens, Brecon

a panache of roses
is the type of exuberance I like in a garden

the fat
buds that rupture along the stem in clusters

stealing the light
from the humped ground dwellers (lesser columbine)

extras
who pad out the scene with tiresome gestures of seasonality

my garden
is an extended plot of beautiful intrigue, technical vigour

when the leading man
leads you to the arbour, where anything might happen, beneath the swag

of petals
the odour of orange-scented blossom, the soft cushion of morning

grasping
amongst the sudden red of leaves, the urgent snow falling

that thorns are tragic, flowers comedic
and a garden

is nature
in a costume, thrown onto a stage and told to play herself (only better)

Flora
Sugar Loaf Mountain, Abergavenny

it's only within thirty feet of the summit
that the mountain starts

until then
a shorn hill shaped like a volcano (the stone far too young for
that to be true)

in the crevices of the rocks
is the flora
that the sheep can't reach

rue-leaved saxifrage, procumbent pearlwort
roseroot, green spleenwort and brittle bladder-fern

which are alpine (if not arctic)
miniatures
astray from fauna and time

as if the *gwyll*
had cast a spell and hid a garden amongst the cracks

though this isn't that type of poem
it's just
that science has so many unspeakable facts

most plants
are actually quite dull
it's the finding of them in unexpected places, that sets the
mind racing

T-Shirt
Glangrwyney

hanging from a tree
as if one day of good weather, was enough for blossom

the wind
frets at the fabric and there's probably a story behind this

but
I wonder if it's my size and too young for me

there are four seasons
and like the leaves that turn upon the tree

I am furled
a flag, purled by the promises of birds

who could take years from me
but, though the shirt is free

I shall leave it upon the tree
half mast, like a rag of Spring

a reminder
that green leaves have in them, the nature of their dying

Yellow Wagtails

these are not yellow wagtails
but the common grey

flashing its belly
as flying (in disguise) to another part of the river

not so much
evolution satisfied

as look
look what I might have been!

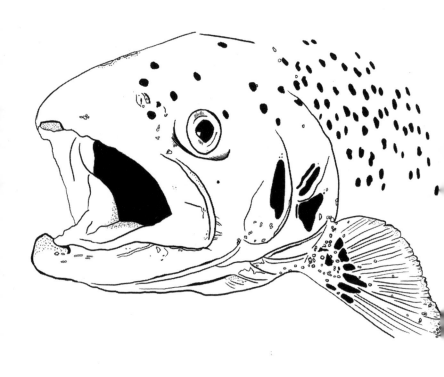

Fishing
Llangynidr Bridge

I don't have the patience to tickle a trout
but in clear water

the fish
are wise to hide beneath stones in the deeper pools

as quickly
the fly whips across the stream

along the imagined arc
of rod and line

I look down from the cutwater
at the spinning reel

the hook
once more waiting

like a false word
baited

an acquired skill that is easy to admire
though the fish

upon the wall
might use a different aphorism

Otters

for a threesome
the otters are making it look easy
slippery like bars of soap

they swim up river
(the moribund sluice)
that powered one water-wheel

and made someone twenty guineas
whilst otters
moved to quieter waters

it looks like a lot of fun
and if I could join them upon the wash stones in the fast-red
stream, I would

stopping only to change my costume
time flows
and the pleasure of skinny-dipping (the dance of the wagtail)

fades
as moiling
I drift onto the sound of the weir

the sparkling cataract
where bones are licked clean
and otters

do not make love on a summer day
but stretch out
upon the balustrade, water-dogs with cheeks full of crayfish

bold tongues
that bring down mountains
I watch from high windows of the felin

the unsleeping stream
that even now
wakes me with romps of otters

Narrow Boat

it's rather like camping
everything must be put back in its place after use

mugs washed at once after the last sip
clothes hung up

that's how all is kept ship shape and shiny
a place for everything and everything in its place

though as you roll out of the narrow bed
mind your head

and don't step on the wine glass
or trip on trousers discarded in haste

in this narrow space
love is a folded blanket and a tidy shelf

an aphorism yet to find its way into romantic literature
though worth a footnote

today
I say nothing and let you be

like a vow I made
to not be alone

we lie together unspeaking
in the bed of spoons we are making

there is scarce time now
to be unkempt

Brynich Aqueduct

the keystone
is the strength of any arch

the trick
of transporting one reach of water over another

the perch and roach
and others of the shallow trench

unaware of their suspension
continue

to feed and scrap
and even procreate (fifty feet up)

as if bricks and limestone
are sediment

and the drop to the river
a water-fall

the art
of snugging one stone against another

is the adaptation of habitat
by thought

an arch carved by a chisel
is still nature

Your Father Said

that if you dawdled on the bridge
the Teg would come for you

turn you
into one of them

you meet your lover
on the green side of the bridge

cold stone soberness
not what you expected from a *cariad*

the water
chases fish around the rocks

and the girl waiting on the other side
scowls at his nerve

your Father said
that God was a gentleman

and easy to forgive
but if you dally on that bridge

you sit on the keystone of the span
watching fish chase hooks

bewitched
by the rush of the river below

Cows

I trudge past the smallest megalith in Wales
then back

to trace my finger
along the furrows and curlicues

which could be Latin
or archaic Welsh, for "may the Gods go with you"

more likely
the recent cattle have sharpened horns upon the stone

leaving behind
their monoglot scratchings, defecating as they did so

which is no surprise
for we have the absurd idea that nature improved, should be grateful

to be trapped in a field
and *enhanced* by cruel and unusual masters

we stand stones and dress them in unnatural poses
like we are not hurting

the cow looks at the stone
and goes about its pneumatic business

Wysg

there are many fish in the river
(trout
 shad and cochgangen)

so many
that the river is cognate (the common brittonic)

but unlike
rivers that flirt with the border (hook, line and sinker)

the water
brooks temptation and stays within its margin

thronged
with the many fish (eog da iawn)

from bog
to the tide of houses

words flowing
from mouth to the many tongues of the sea

The Heron

stands
stone-still
like a figure upon an enamel badge

heralding
not much
beside the swiftness of the river

this season
he wears a grey suit with black and cream accessories

as natural
as anything can be in nature

just then
he almost moved

not so much standing still

as evolution
morphing in the slowest of ratios

Standing Still

A cattled street
of chewed over straw, then
the sudden iron rail

I have stood still
all my life, asked for little
and received a gradual education
of nuance

others walked or
ran to the silver trains
making a market of their
wide open souls.

I have stayed
slow and accidental
and hidden behind trees
and built a temper

Pasg

the rain began
I put on my waterproofs (bright yellow)

you couldn't miss me, walking to the cathedral
over water

the rain stops

I keep the waterproofs on, make myself obvious
like a clown

the bells ring out and the town takes cover

tradition
being for the very hard of believing

the rain begins
I put on waterproofs (bright yellow)

what I was, I remain (and am)

Poem Against the Welsh
after Robert Bly

the best of a bad job
is seen all over Wales

the ruined window
the sheep upon the thirteenth green

and somewhere up a mountain
Owain Glyndŵr snatched a strange kind of victory, by dying
obscurely

all conquered nations are sensitive
and there is a barter between motor cars and *mafon duon*

the Saxons
who stare at beauty spots, when in small, ugly towns

the extravagance of Welsh life
goes on

it is good to be poor
and listen to the wind in the trees

it is also good
to pull your finger out   and do   some   thing

A Horse Galloping Through Brecon Museum

before the capture
of silver upon glass

it was a lucky guess
by the artist

to paint the correct gait
of a horse

the life-size portrait
of the Marquess of Bute's

stud stallion
an arrested study of proportion

action
the feisty hero of the track

ready to leap
from the wall

intuition
a better wager than the photographic plate

that stable in its nitrate
repeats and does not create

To a Bronze Statue of the Duke of Wellington

written in the nearest pub; Brecon/Aberhonddu

what is he doing
up there upon a pedestal

blown
out of all proportion

green now
the hollow bronze

has a glorious view from Brecon to the border
O England

you don't learn do you
imposing the metal Duke upon market square

later
I found that the statue was erected

by a gallant admirer
Evan Thomas by name (a local man)

which showed me
that opinion is often ignorance in translation

somebody buy me a drink
I can't stand it

Rats

I am
the God beyond the plasterboard

a diplomatic zone
where at night I am woken

by the bantering and scurrying
of others

I place my bait
in the space that separates

my mind
a fierce tyrant of wakefulness

I sleep
whilst my revenge

scythes
through the furtive passages

like a pejorative sense of fear
I am

my own fantoum
and the house smells of nothing but rats

Cath
after Mircea Ivanescu

where is the cat?

if we go out
we would see only his shadow

he uses his whiskers
to see

we whisper
where is the cat?

we have given him food
and rats

why does he stay out?

is he watching us
from under the white iron bridge?

is he dead
amongst kite feathers?

why do I call
when you live in silence?

Lay-By, A470, Storey Arms Pass

late
so five minutes won't make a difference

it's raining
chunks

the wipers
taking a breather at the ten o'clock position

this road is closed
snow covering the contours like spilt emulsion

and glaciation
is pouring newly over the crags and darrens

I consider
sleeping in my car

whilst the snow and ice
grind out a new level

five minutes
won't make a difference

Standing Stone

slanted
  like a ship's prow
    ready
      to be carved

the menhir stands
    like a sketch
        amongst
            cows

like an apothecary's
          sign
            (health and a cure
            for sadness found here)

a nine foot
      geodetic finger-post
            pointing toward

a fold of the optic nerve
        a yew
            growing by a waterfall

older
    than forestry
        older than the fields

a skewed
      polygon
          holding
              ground

Hess

upon the Skirrid
you can follow in the steps of Rudolph Hess

through the strident bracken
skirting others

I imagine him as a Romantic figure firmly gazing
upon Sugar Loaf

silently cursing his inaction
but like a true trooper gallantly performing for his captors

a melodrama
written by Goethe and scored by Wagner

whilst a thousand miles away
German soldiers are wiping the sweat from dead eyes

he is killing time
burying notes beneath the stones of the asylum

hoping that a bargain can be made
from vain deeds and the vainer thoughts of Nietzsche

5G

when I got
to seventeen hundred feet

I was surprised
to find I had a strong, powerful signal

soon
I was taking photographs and posting updates

four hours
have passed since I stepped on the mountain

and I don't see
the nettle hiding bracken

but scouting
I do see the way of water

running
four different ways down the darren

trumpets blowing
like the charging Gods of the Mabinogion

this is not something I can put on social media
maybe in a poem

Pen y Fan

on a track
no wider than a sheep

I am defacing
not decorating the scenery

and I should have turned back
before
my ambition unroped itself from my abilities

above
upon thermals (above the soaring peaks)

kites
are showing how feathers are the way to get around

I sucker myself
to the whorls of the mountain

turn
and take in the terrifying compass

Windflowers

I stand upon the bank of the Wysg
the anemones
like notes (folded) white (though some streaked with lavender)
torn

for the weather is feminine
she changes
like punctuation
the meaning (of words,written)

I am
confetti, spent petals
tit-bits
for wrens and worms

when pleasure
was the least of my motif, that runs long the bank of the river
I loved

like the dainty work of a bleeding foot
dashing
between lovers (beauty multiplied by itself)

the anemones
like notes (folded) white (streaked with lavender) poison

when between lovers
love
is divided

Here

should I come into money
I won't
travel

I've only just got
here

to gamble
home
against a sweeping view of paradise islands under an azure sky

is risky
as one grows older and walking home at dusk thoughts
turn

to how time passes
like an unsought obligation to the unfound and unseen

and to pack one's belongings in a case and fly seems an awful bother
a flimsy sort of dream

here
I will cease my roving and stay the knowing eye

grow familiar
and watch the world go by

Old Fools Are Babes Again

old
more years than I remember

I've decided to ask
my daughters

who
would most like me to live with them

they discuss
my vices

the likely
rate of degeneration

I offer
my estate for my lodging

and *will*
sign any papers

how long
will the corpus outlive the cerebrum

ten years?
twenty? thirty?

Water

catching water
always leads to a cacophony

never mute
water talks as it spouts or fountains

from mossy lips
to the drum of the barrel

murmuring like a cherub
or roaring like a freshwater Neptune

who opened his mouth to yawn
and was surprised

by a deluge of vowels
that kept on flowing

O, if only my hands
could catch what the water is saying

Wysg - *Usk, River*
Brycheiniog - *Former Kingdom becoming Brecknockshire, also Brecon*
Llyn - *Lake*
Bwlch - *place name, generally a gap or mountain pass*
Hiraeth - *yearning for home*
Gwyll - *ghosts, spirits, night wanderers*
Glangrwyney - *village near Crickhowell*
Teg - *Fairy*
Cariad - *Darling, love interest*
Cochgangen - *Chub*
Eog da iawn - *Very good salmon*
Pasg - *Easter*
Owain Glyndŵr - *Welsh leader c. 1359 – c. 1415*
Mafon duon - *blackberries; colloquial name for tourists arriving in September after the school holidays*
Skirrid - *Eastern outlier of the Black Mountains 486m/1,594ft*
Mabinogion - *A collection of Welsh texts c1350-1410*